#DOGBUTT

AN OFF-COLOR ADULT COLORING BOOK FOR DOG LOVERS

Want free goodies?
Email us at freebies@honeybadgercoloring.com

@honeybadgercoloring

Honey Badger Coloring

Shop our other books at
www.honeybadgercoloring.com

Wholesale distribution through Ingram Content Group
www.ingramcontent.com/publishers/distribution/wholesale

For questions and customer service, email us at
support@honeybadgercoloring.com

FREE PDF DOWNLOAD

OF THIS BOOK

DOWNLOAD CODE:

BUTT739

www.honeybadgercoloring.com/dog

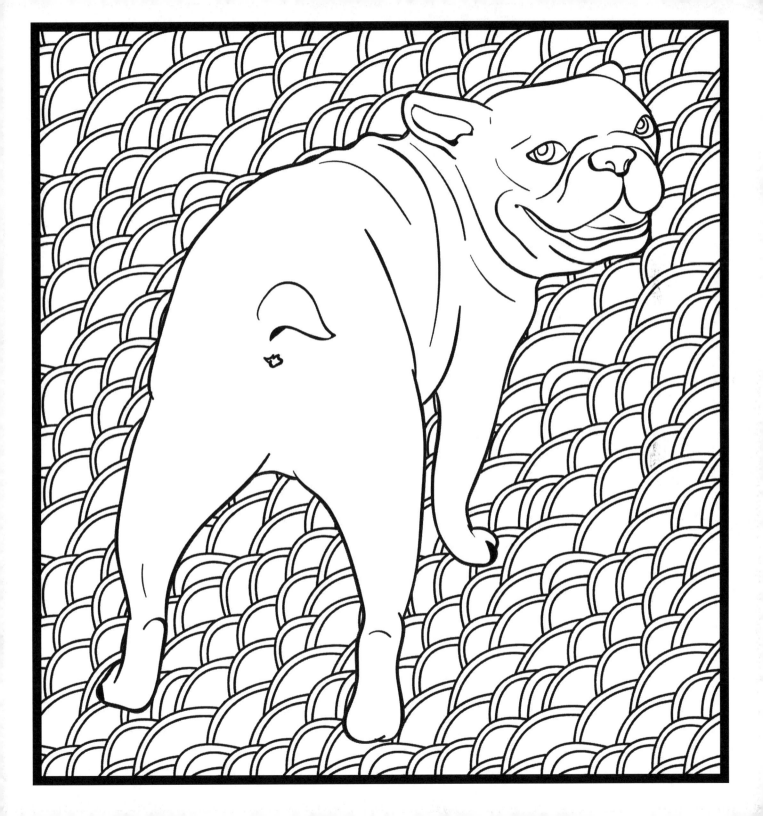

FREE PDF DOWNLOAD

OF THIS BOOK

DOWNLOAD CODE:

BUTT739

www.honeybadgercoloring.com/dog

Want free goodies?
Email us at freebies@honeybadgercoloring.com

@honeybadgercoloring

Honey Badger Coloring

Shop our other books at
www.honeybadgercoloring.com

Wholesale distribution through Ingram Content Group
www.ingramcontent.com/publishers/distribution/wholesale

For questions and customer service, email us at
support@honeybadgercoloring.com

Manufactured by Amazon.ca
Bolton, ON

15203045R00044